HOSTETLER

# BIG TRACKS, LITTLE TRACKS

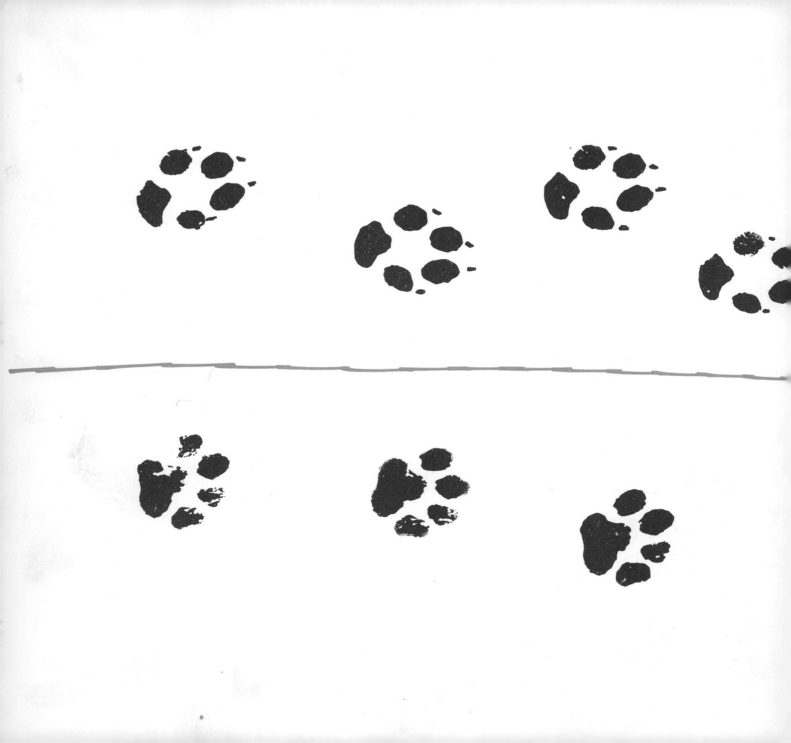

# BIG TRACKS, LITTLE TRACKS

BY **FRANKLYN M. BRANLEY** AND ILLUSTRATED BY **LEONARD KESSLER**

THOMAS Y. CROWELL COMPANY · NEW YORK

# LET'S-READ-AND-FIND-OUT BOOKS

SPECIAL ADVISER: Dr. Roma Gans
*Professor Emeritus of Childhood Education*
*Teachers College, Columbia University*

EDITOR: Dr. Franklyn M. Branley
*Coordinator of Educational Services*
*American Museum-Hayden Planetarium*
*Consultant on science in elementary education*

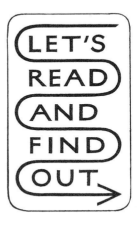

LET'S
READ
AND
FIND
OUT

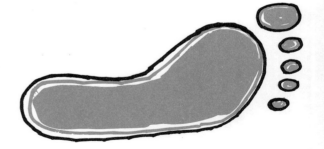

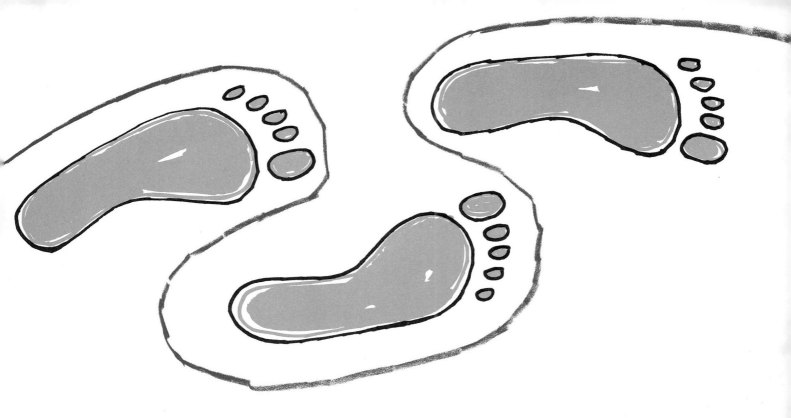

Who was here?
Who made these tracks?
Was it a dog?
Was it a cat?
Was it a boy or girl?

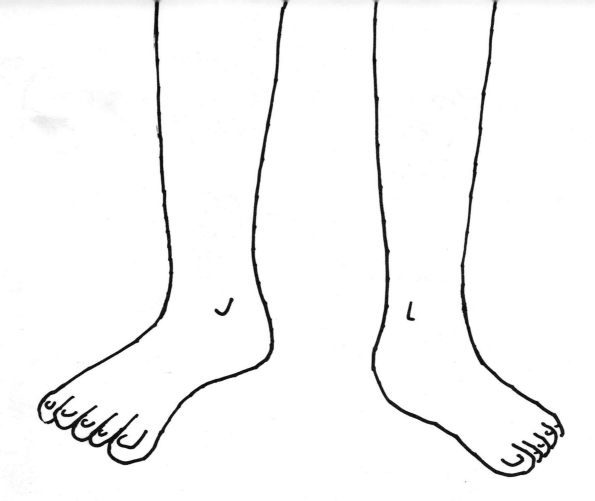

It must have been a boy or girl.
The boy or girl had no shoes on.

You can make your own tracks.
When you take a bath, put your wet feet on a piece
of paper.

Step on it. Do not slide on the paper. You made footprints.

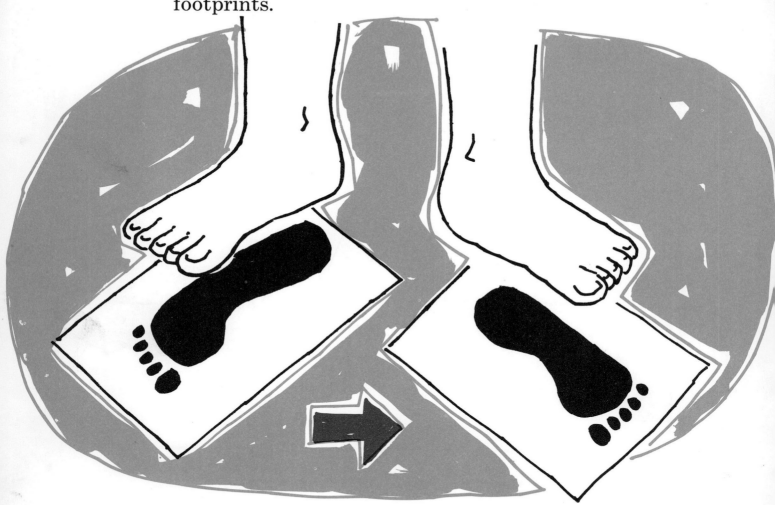

They look like this.

Here are more footprints.
An animal made these footprints.
Do you know what animal made them?
They were made by——

A DOG.

A little dog made these footprints.

Here are more footprints.
They are like the little dog's footprints, but they are
    bigger.
A big dog made these footprints.

The big dog runs after the little dog.

The footprints they make look like this.

Here are more footprints.
They were not made by a little dog.
They were not made by a big dog.

What animal made them? Can you guess?
They were made by——

A RABBIT.

Rabbit tracks in the snow look like this.

Rabbit tracks in the desert look like this.

Here are more footprints.
They are not rabbit tracks.
What animal made them? Can you guess?
They were made by——

A CAT.
A cat jumps and climbs.
A cat walks on top of things.
Cat tracks look like this.

The big dog runs after the cat.
The little dog runs after the cat.
The cat runs after the rabbit.
The rabbit runs away.

The tracks of the big dog, the little dog, the cat, and
the rabbit look like this.

Let's look for tracks.
Some tracks are easy to find.
It is easy to see tracks made

by a man with no shoes on,

by a man with shoes on,

by a woman with shoes on,

by a woman with no shoes on,

by children with shoes on,

by children with no shoes on,

by big dogs,

by little dogs,

by cats,

by rabbits.

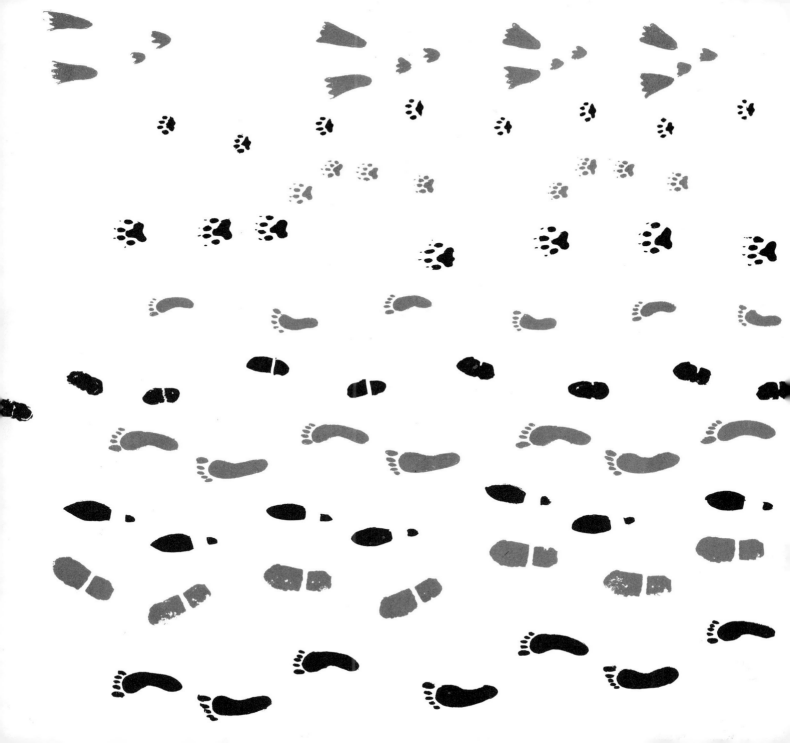

Have you ever seen bird tracks?

A robin was here.

A duck was here.

A chicken was here.

Tracks like these are easy to find.

Some tracks are hard to find.
Does this look like the track of an animal?
It is.
It was made by——

A WORM.

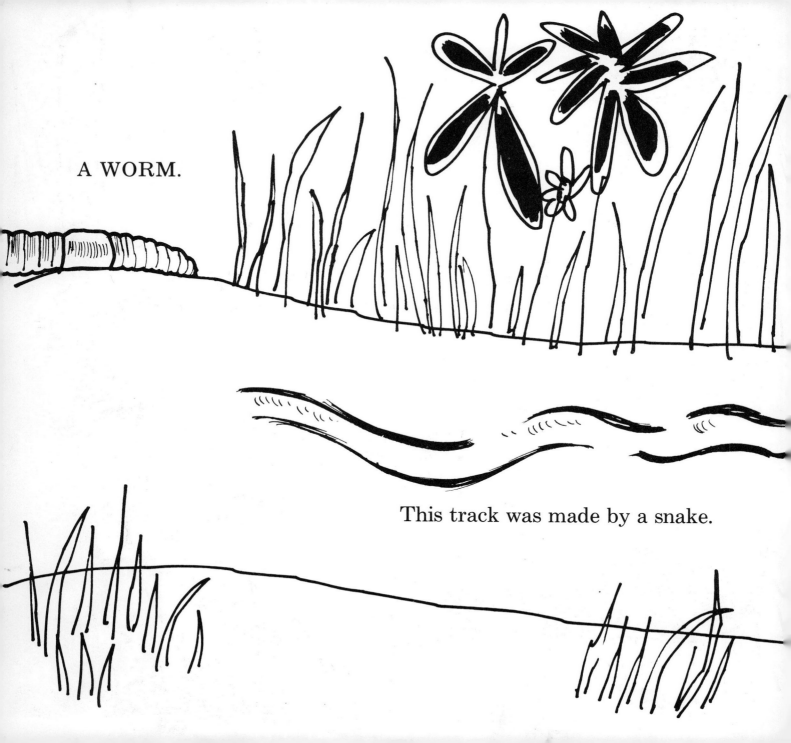

This track was made by a snake.

Did you ever see tracks like these?
They do not look like tracks at all, but they are.
These tracks were made by large ants.
We cannot see the tracks made by small ants.

Here are tracks made by animals.
Do you know the animals that made them?

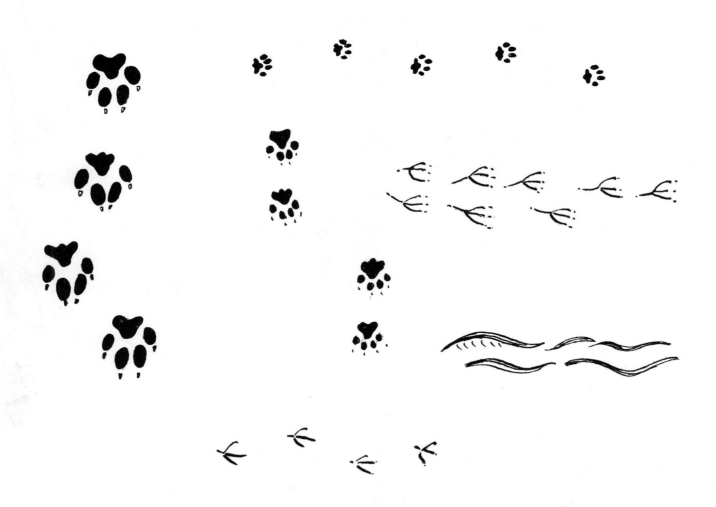

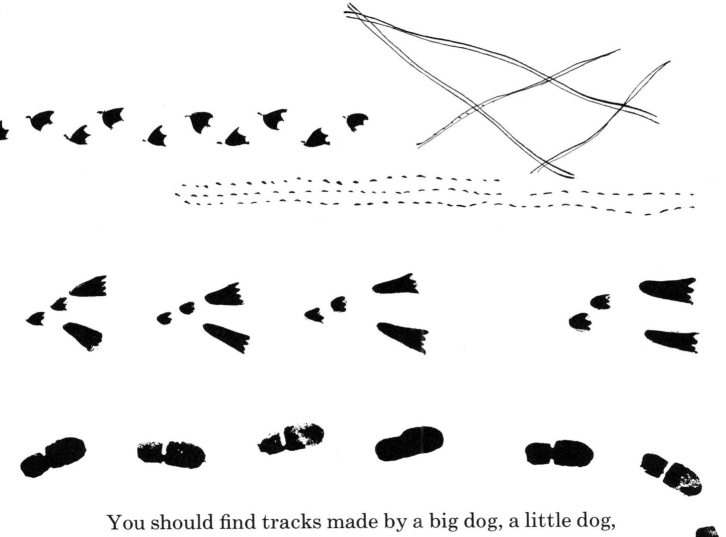

You should find tracks made by a big dog, a little dog,
a rabbit, a cat, a chicken, a robin, a duck, a worm,
a snake, an ant, and YOU!

Here are the animals and the tracks they made.

See what animal tracks you can find.

You can see tracks in wet sand, in snow, in soft earth.

Sometimes you can see wet tracks on rocks.

You cannot see dry tracks on rocks.

From animal tracks we can find out
    if the animal was big or little,
    if the animal walked or ran,
    if the animal ran after another animal.
We can find out many things.

Why don't you look for animal tracks?
Why don't you see what you can find out?

## ABOUT THE AUTHOR

FRANKLYN M. BRANLEY is Astronomer at the American Museum–Hayden Planetarium where he directs the diverse educational program. For many years he has helped children learn scientific facts and principles at an early age without impairing their sense of wonder about the world they live in. Before coming to the Planetarium, Dr. Branley taught science at many grade levels including the lower elementary grades, high school, college, and graduate school.

He lives with his wife and two daughters in Woodcliff Lake, New Jersey.

## ABOUT THE ARTIST

LEONARD KESSLER has left his tracks in many places. After working as a teacher, clarinetist, display artist, and program director of a children's camp, he has settled down to being a designer and commercial artist and the author and illustrator of books for children.

Born in Akron, Ohio, he moved to Pittsburgh at an early age. After earning his degree from the Carnegie Institute of Technology in Pittsburgh, Mr. Kessler moved to New York City. He lives now with his wife and two children in Rockland County, New York.